FOR I KNOW THE PLANS
I HAVE FOR YOU,"
DECLARES THE LORD,
"PLANS TO PROSPER YOU
AND NOT TO HARM YOU,
PLANS TO GIVE YOU
HOPE AND A FUTURE

JEREMIAH 29:11

This book is dedicated to my big sister, best friend, and twin Crystal Kimbrel (Krystalized Kustoms)

When things go wrong as they sometimes will,
When the road you're trudging seems all up hill,
When the funds are low and the debts are high
And you want to smile, but you have to sigh,
When care is pressing you down a bit,
Rest if you must, but don't you quit.
Life is strange with its twists and turns
As every one of us sometimes learns
And many a failure comes about
When he might have won had he stuck it out;
Don't give up though the pace seems slow—
You may succeed with another blow.
Success is failure turned inside out—
The silver tint of the clouds of doubt,
And you never can tell just how close you are,
It may be near when it seems so far;
So stick to the fight when you're hardest hit—
It's when things seem worst that you must not quit.

After all is said and done, the one skill that keeps the lights on in your business is sales. A company that can't sell its products or services is quickly going out of business. Regardless of your craft, even artists, software developers, writers and just about everyone needs selling skills to get by in the business world.

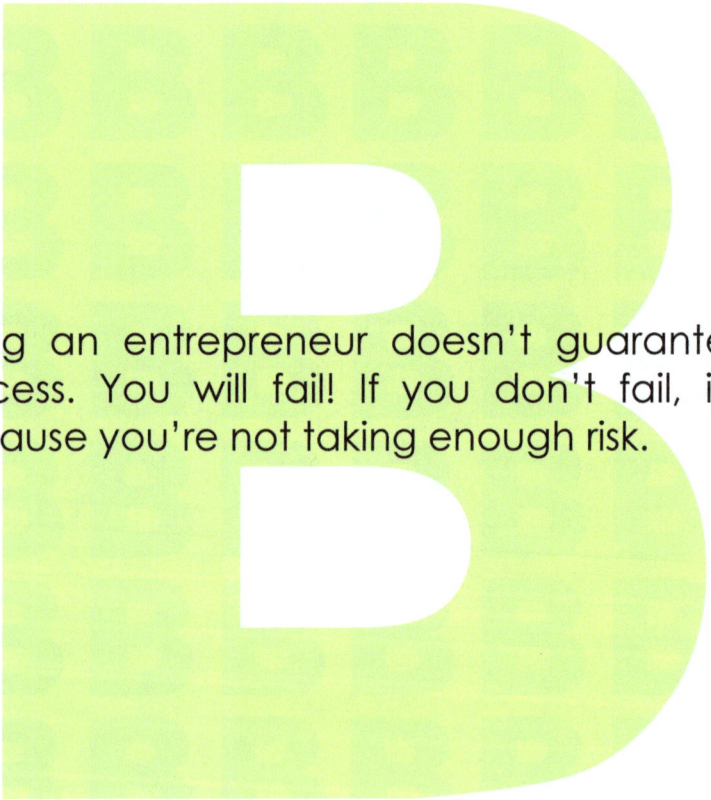

Being an entrepreneur doesn't guarantee success. You will fail! If you don't fail, it's because you're not taking enough risk.

Communication is Key! Your business can quickly go from good to bad when communication lacks purpose, clarity and impact. In fact, effective communication can revolutionize an idea, breathe new life into a product or brand.

Don't take your customers for granted. You might have customers who are interested in your product or service, but if you don't listen to their complaints, you soon will have no customers. Take your customers seriously, treat their complaints with respect, and listen. You might think you're giving them value, but they may not agree.

Entrepreneurs should never turn down a conversation. When you're overworked, it's easy to think you don't have time for coffee with person A or a phone call with person B. In reality, everyone has something to teach you. You just have to be willing to be taught.

Fear stops action. Entrepreneurs have to be able to pivot and quickly take action when they see an opportunity or recognize a mistake.

Get a job if you have to. You will not lose your will to be an entrepreneur for doing so.

However, it's important to understand that to be a successful entrepreneur, you need to eat, sleep, and breathe what your business is about. To be clear, this doesn't mean you need to work weekends. However, it does mean you need to obsess over what your business is about and, well...probably work weekends (at least in the beginning).

It's OK to look up to another entrepreneur and have a "healthy" jealousy of what he/she has accomplished, just make sure this drives you harder and doesn't take away from your plans to push ahead.

Just like marriages and Hollywood careers, businesses fail all the time. The secret to success as an entrepreneur is to get back on your feet again, pick up the pieces and apply what you've painfully learned so that you'll get different results the next time.

Know when to say No! Not all business is good business. The more I said no, the faster I grew. So turn down work that doesn't fit your mission or expertise. Work with customers who help sharpen your brand and reputation, offer repeat business, or serve as referrals.

Lack of the ability to manage finances exposes you to the risk of becoming unsustainable, which often leads to bankruptcy, regret and going back to a full-time job. Develop discipline and prudence, especially when it comes to purchases for personal and business purposes.

Making promises and not delivering is a quick way to lose your business.
In contrast, successful entrepreneurs exceed expectations.If you deliver more than you promised, you're sure to have satisfied customers, investors, and business partners.

Network, network, network! Meet everyone you come into contact with and have a short chat. You never know who you're sitting next to and what connections or resources they might be able to offer you. You might find a new connection while shopping at D&G's Klassy Designs Pop Up Shops, you might meet your next business partner in an elevator on your way to a meeting, and you just never know who's sitting next to you on the bus.

Open your mind and read about successful businesses. Take in the wealth of knowledge that's been provided by successful entrepreneurs such as Steve Jobs and the personalities from Shark Tank. A successful business plan does not have to be a book. A 10-page plan is digestible yet long enough to include everything you need to start.

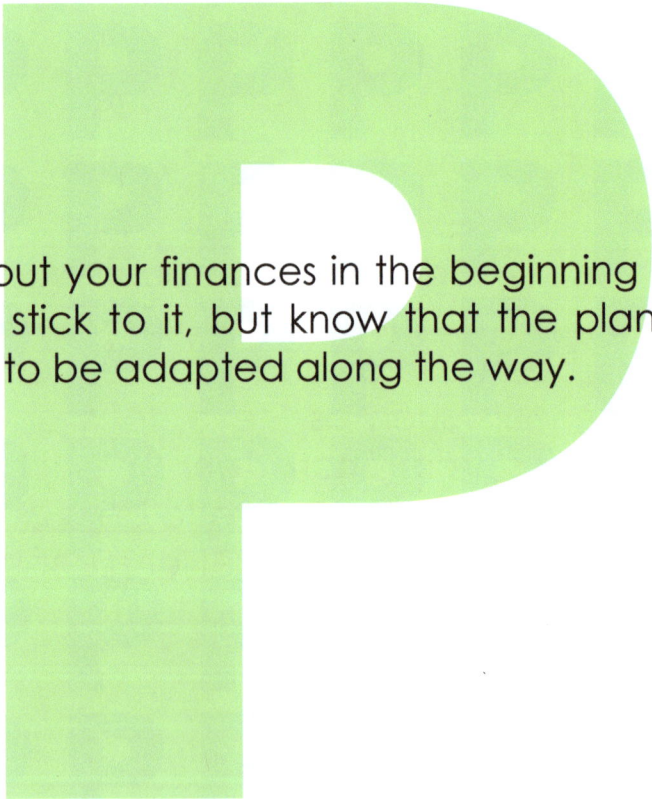

Plan out your finances in the beginning and try to stick to it, but know that the plan will have to be adapted along the way.

Quality time with Friends and family is important, those will be the people that will keep you humble

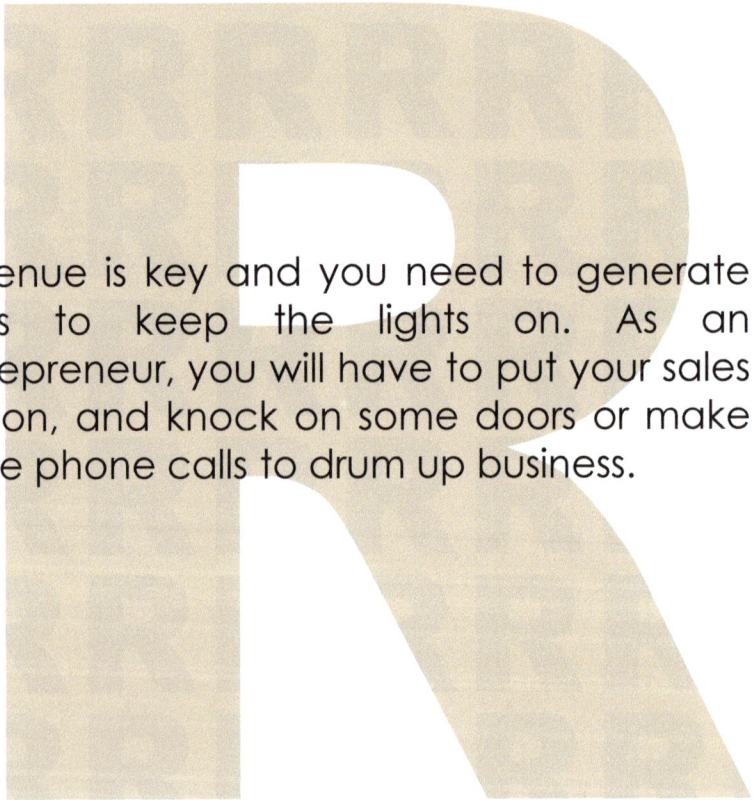

Revenue is key and you need to generate sales to keep the lights on. As an entrepreneur, you will have to put your sales hat on, and knock on some doors or make some phone calls to drum up business.

Self Promote! Know your business, know some key stats, and have your 15-second elevator pitch polished and ready to go. Then, when someone asks you about your business, you can promote it factually and quickly.

There will be long nights, you will work weekends and may even have some days where you don't sleep at all. Work while your competitors sleep in order to get ahead! A key point is sharing what your customers are saying about your business. Tell the good and the bad.

Uplift your brothers and sisters that are entrepreneurs. Sometimes the person who need help look nothing like the person who need help.

Values that an entrepreneur needs are attributes such as honesty, passion, determination, and confidence. No one likes to do business with people that are arrogant, selfish, dismissive and egotistic. Any business venture is a reflection of the entrepreneur's personal values, attitudes, and beliefs.

When choosing your partners and team members, always remember that you can teach skills, but you can't teach character.

X- Factor a circumstance, quality, or person that has a strong but unpredictable influence. It's an unknown or unexplained element that makes something more interesting or valuable

You don't determine what a good product is. Only your customer does. And if they don't like your product, it's a bad product. Period. In others words, the customer is always right.

Zeal is needed for Entrepreneurs. It is dedication or enthusiasm for something. If you have zeal, you're willing, energized, and motivated to do the work.